If I File It, Can I Find It?

STRATEGIES FOR ORGANIZING YOUR OFFICE AND YOUR THINKING

by Sue McMillin

A FEW CLIENTS INCLUDE:
AOL | AT&T | Boeing | Conoco Phillips
Kodak | Marriott | Met Life | Proctor & Gamble
Xerox | Homeland Security

WHAT CLIENTS
ARE SAYING

"Wow! What a difference you have made in our lives... you helped us find more than 40% space in our department alone! Our productivity has increased and your FileMAP® System works. Thank you for making us a better department."

— Debi M., Floyd Memorial Hospital

"Our entire group is so much more efficient... a life changing experience"

— Stacy S., 5/3 Bank

"I do not believe that I have ever learned so much useful information in one day. Your system works!... Personally, I am delighted with my new office... It is a real morale booster... Please do not hesitate to use us as a reference and I would be willing to speak with anyone on your behalf."

— Jane M., Fairfax Hospital

"Terrific! Sue is an excellent speaker... Very informative"

— Robert W., Northern KY University

"Your seminar and time have been well worth the time and effort expended... For the first time in over three years in this position, I can keep up and manage what is coming my way on a daily basis."

— Susan C., Kodak

"My whole way of thinking and living has been changed! The five tips you recommended for organizing a desk were fantastic and I am using them. I truly have Time to Spare, I love it and I feel so together!"

— Steve G., Citizens Against Crime

"My office has been transformed from a place people stared at in mock horror to amazement... It's amazing how an office can be transformed in one day."

— Kevin G., Cable and Wireless

ADDITIONAL CLIENTS

CORPORATIONS
3M | AMS | Cable & Wireless | Eli Lilly | Fannie Mae | Ashland Oil
Gannett | Honeywell | Intel | MCI | Steelcase | Toyota | Trane
5/3 Bank | Pacific Bell | PricewaterhouseCoopers

GOVERNMENT
EPA | NOAA | USDA | US Courts | HUD | DOE | PTO | DHS

HOSPITALS
Georgetown Medical (DC) | Fairfax Hospital (VA)
St. Joseph Hospital (KY) | Floyd Memorial Hospital (IN)
National Institutes of Health (MD) | Boulder Hospital (CO)

ASSOCIATIONS
ABA | APA | APPA | NEA

OTHER GROUPS
Northern KY University | Hillenmeyer Nurseries
Mary Kay | James Gray Company

CHRISTIAN ORGANIZATIONS
Campus Crusade for Christ | Navigators | World Vision | YWAM
Young Life | New Life Church (CO) | Church on the Move (OK)
Prison Fellowship | Focus on the Family

CHRISTIAN CAMPS
Shocco Springs Baptist Conference Center (AL)
Camp Eagle (TX)

PUBLISHED IN

The Washington Post Magazine | *USAir Magazine*
Investor's Business Daily | *Changing Times Magazine*
Focus on the Family Magazine | *Brio Magazine*
KY Living | *Godly Business Woman Magazine*

For quantity purchases of this book or other books written
by this author or for information regarding seminars or
consulting services in your home or office, see the contact
information below.

Sue McMillin, President
With Time To Spare

E-MAIL
Sue@WithTimeToSpare.com

VISIT OUR WEB SITE AT
www.WithTimeToSpare.com

OTHER BOOKS BY THIS AUTHOR

They Could Be Giants
Taken By Surprise

TABLE OF CONTENTS

PART I: HOW TO ORGANIZE YOUR THINKING
21 Paradigms to Organize Your Thinking,
Time, Tasks, and Things

TABLE OF CONTENTS (continued)

PART II: HOW TO ORGANIZE YOUR OFFICE

INTRODUCTION

I have been in the business of assisting corporations, government agencies, non-profit organizations, hospitals, manufacturing, small businesses, individuals, and churches to become better organized since 1982, and **I have seen everything!** There was the government agent in Washington, D.C., who had two drawers of napkins and the corporate manager in Virginia who had 11 glue sticks. Then there was the pastor in Maryland who had a pile of papers on his desk that was four feet tall. The only way he could work at his desk was to stand up. Finally, there was the brilliant, beautiful congressional worker who had 50 tubes of lipstick and 119 eyeliners. We have too much stuff, and it's blocking out light and air.

But this is not just a book on how to transform your office, it's a book about changing your thinking. To become better organized in your office and even your home and life, you must change the way you think.

As I have traveled across this beautiful country and worked with every conceivable kind of person, I have noticed a pattern, a consistent paradigm, or way of thinking, that permeates the minds and hearts of many of the clients mentioned above. One of the reasons my clients struggle with disorganization is because of the way they think. True, sometimes they struggle because of their lack of training, or they just don't take the time to organize. Mostly, though, it is how they think that gets them into trouble. When I directly affect their thinking and train them in the art of organizing, they stay organized. Therefore, the following maxim is true:

When you think properly about getting organized, you will become organized. The only prerequisite to getting organized is the willingness to change. Once you are willing to change, the training, the motivation, and the time to do it will flow your way.

It's our thinking that needs to change, not just our training or our schedule or our children or our habits or our spouses or whatever excuse we have for why we are not organized. When we eliminate old, outdated ways of thinking and change our paradigms (perspectives) about getting organized, we will be well on the road to a new way of looking at ourselves; we will begin the process of organizing, and we will stay organized.

PARADIGMS & PARADIGM SHIFTS

Nowadays we are hearing so much about paradigms. What are paradigms? Someone once said, "Why, it's two dimes!" Actually, a paradigm is a perspective or a mindset. It is how you perceive things, or, we might say, it is the grid through which you view your world. Let me give you some paradigms and tell you who said them. Thomas Watson, the founder of IBM®, said, "I think there is a world market for about five computers." Thomas Edison said, "The phonograph is not of any commercial value." All these were paradigms, statements about how these individuals felt or perceived their products. Thank heavens they changed or made a paradigm shift. Can you imagine where we would be today if we had no computers or televisions?

In my seminar, I have before and after slides of clients whom I have worked with. One of these slides shows a client who has on his desk a small sign that says, "This clutter is my bread and butter." I was able to help him reorganize his office, but I was not able to motivate him to change his thinking, so in a few weeks, his office slipped back into its original chaos. In order to get organized, you must look at how you are thinking. Perhaps it's not just the fact that you need help with the organizing process or that you have never been trained in the skill of organizing. Perhaps it's that your perspective needs adjusting; your paradigm needs to change or shift.

In the following paradigms, I deal with our thinking. This is not just a book on reorganizing our stuff; it's a book on reorganizing our perspectives. Once the thinking has been transformed, the reorganizing process is a snap. As one of my colleagues says, it's organizing from the inside out. If you change your paradigm, then your home, office, kids, time, and life will forever be ordered, and you will become a more productive person. You will be more productive in work, at play, at home, and in your relationships.

I will share with you some specific paradigms, how some people think and perceive their environments. Then I will define for you the paradigm shifts that they must make to get organized. The professionals say that it takes 21 days to change a thought process or habit; therefore, I am offering 21 paradigms and their shifts. Read one per day and spend the day pondering that shift. Begin applying the new shift immediately and watch how it affects your time and place. Whether you want a newly reorganized clothes closet, your office staff to be more productive, or your kids to clean their rooms, this book will help you.

Becoming organized has wonderful benefits. It brings a sense of stability and peace. Where there is order, there is peace, and real order liberates rather than confines (an actual paradigm). Becoming organized has set many of my clients free. It will set you free, too.

This book will give you a step-by-step method for organizing your thinking and your professional and home office. It's divided into the following sections:

PART I: HOW TO ORGANIZE YOUR THINKING.

- 21 paradigms to organize your thinking, time, tasks and things

PART II: HOW TO ORGANIZE YOUR OFFICE.

- The 5-Step Procedure. Through this Procedure, you will transform your office into a work of art. These 5 steps can organize not only your desk, but also your home and any place else that needs organizing.
- What the office should look like. I will discuss my innovative FileMAP® System, how to organize all your supplies, my 3D Process to organize all your loose papers, and what to do with your books/ resources.
- The actual approach of where to start, giving you a step-by-step plan to excavate your desk.
- How to organize your computer files and e-mails.
- Creative and snappy ideas on maintaining the organization.

In just a few short days, you will have a new desk, office and a renewed mind.

PART I

How to Organize Your Thinking

———— ———— ———— ———— ———— ————

21 Paradigms to Organize Your Thinking, Time, Tasks and Things

PARADIGM #1:

"I don't have time to organize."

[PARADIGM SHIFT]
"I organize to have time."

"I don't have time to organize." Have you ever said that to yourself in the heat of frustration? We live out that maxim in so many ways. We are constantly looking for our keys, yet we don't take the time to create a snappy, simple system with a place to put our keys so we can always find them. How about our spices? Constantly, we shuffle through the jars to find the spice we need. If we would take the time and put the spices into a system, we could instantly find the spice we want when we need it. We are buried by our good intentions. "I am saving all this paperwork, because there are some great ideas I might want to do one of these days." We never get to it; the paperwork mounts up; we shuffle and unstack, search through and swear over it. Yet it does not occur to us to stop work to establish a system for our mail so that when we do need a certain piece of paper. . . you get the picture.

Here is a classic story regarding one of my clients. I was in Indiana working at a corporation, and upon entering an office to start my coaching, I noticed a pile of neatly stacked papers in the corner. The pile was about three feet tall, and my client said that it was a monthly report that he referred to about seven times a day. When I asked him to find the March 17 report, it took him three minutes. Multiply three minutes by seven and you get about 20 minutes a day that he wasted going through work to get to work. I suggested that we organize the report into a simple system so he could access any report in seconds. Do you know what he said? "I don't have time."

This is a fabulous example of how we waste precious time operating under the wrong paradigm. Needless to say, we took the time to set up a system. (It took about 20 minutes.) We just set up 31 hanging files numbered 1-31 and placed each report in its corresponding number. The March 3 report went into the number 3 file, and so on. Now when he needs to reference March 17, he goes to the file numbered 17 and pulls out the report in three seconds — 20 minutes saved a day. He grosses (probably) $100,000 a year. That's $50 an hour or about $1 a minute. Twenty dollars a day multiplied by 244 workdays equals about $5,000 a year that I saved his company, simply by setting up a system for his reports.

You organize to have time.

Point made.

PARADIGM #2:

"I am constantly un-
stacking stuff to
get to stuff."

[PARADIGM SHIFT]
"Don't go through your work to get to your work."

Do you want to discover instantly if you need to reorganize any area in your office or home? Ask yourself the question, "Am I going through my work to get to my work?" Whenever I ask this question in my seminars, I get major groans from the audience. "That's exactly what I am doing all day long" is their response. If you are going through your work to get to your work, then you are costing your company money and wasting precious time when you could be working and producing, or perhaps relaxing with your family.

For example, in your office, do you move your papers from one location to another because you do not have enough work space to do your work? Are you piling your work files and then having to unstack them in order to find the file you need? In your home, are you lifting three pans to get to your skillet? Are you moving countless knickknacks in order to dust? In your bedroom, are you constantly shuffling through your socks to find the correct pair? If you can say yes to any of the above, you are going through your work to get to your work, and thus, you are doubling your work.

Look at what this may be costing your company regarding its bottom line. Let's say you gross $60,000 a year. That translates into about 30 dollars an hour. If you spend precious time going through your work to get to your work, then you are probably losing, conservatively, 30 minutes a day. That means the time wasted in a year will cost your company about $15 dollars a day or about $3,600 in lost productivity per employee. All this because you are simply looking for your work. Perhaps this thought still doesn't motivate you to change. Well, what is going through your work to get to your work doing to your psyche? You stew because you constantly misplace your files, or your keys, or whatever. Your marriage is negatively affected, because now both parties have to stop their normal routines to search for what was misplaced. You get angry at yourself once again and promise yourself once again that you are going to get organized, but life swallows your time and off you go, never stopping to address the real problem. Consequently, this dance is repeated over and over.

Take some time during your workday and notice if you are searching for your work. If you are, take some more time to reorganize and establish a system for your files, paperwork, or whatever needs adjusting. You will feel better about yourself, save your company a lot of money, and save yourself a lot of energy.

PARADIGM #3:

"I can never seem
to finish anything.
I get distracted so
easily."

"Finish fully a project or finish a portion of what you start."

One of my clients, who calls herself the Queen of Distractions, relayed this story to me. She starts her day by vacuuming her house. As she is focusing on the vacuuming and accomplishing this task, she accidentally turns over a plant. As she picks up the mess, she realizes that she has failed to water her plants this week, so she heads for the kitchen to get some water. As she is filling her water jug, she notices that her breakfast dishes are caked with a hard crust and filling the sink, so she stops her watering and begins to wash her dishes. On and on throughout her day, she repeats this habit, and consequently, when her husband walks in from work and asks her how her day was, she knows for sure she has worked hard all day, but she doesn't have a thing to show for it. She has started but not finished a single task.

When I tell this story in my seminars, I get nervous laughter from the audience. Are we being distracted to the point of never finishing what we start? Nobody cares a whit about the projects we start; they only want to see the finished results. It does not matter how many times we start something, because success only comes when we finish.

When I was growing up in the hills of Kentucky, I lived in a rural area. My town consisted of 30 homes, about 80 people, and my father ran the country grocery store. It was the hub of the community. I sacked groceries, pumped gas, sliced bologna, and played checkers with all the men that came in every night for a spit and a chew as they sat around the old pot-belly stove, playing cards and talking about their "old ladies." My mom insisted that I get involved in 4-H, a rural-school organization that taught Christian character through projects like entomology, raising cattle, sewing, home improvement, and so forth. The one thing that she insisted upon was that I finish any project that I started, and she meant it. Every, and I mean every, project that I started, I finished. I still do to this day. My mother embedded this work ethic into my very pores. Thank heaven! It's a joy to experience.

Finishing brings relief, eliminates guilt, brings closure, and liberates your spirit. So before you start, count the cost, analyze the steps, plan your strategy, and leave ample time to finish the project.

PARADIGM #4:

"I'll just put it
here in case I need
it... I'll just stick
it here for now."

[PARADIGM SHIFT]
"Put things away, not down."

My mom used to say that when I came home from school, she could track me all the way through our country store, into the house, and clear into my room by following my "droppings."

First went the satchel, then my coat, then the dress (ugh, we had to wear dresses to school), then the shoes, and finally, all the rest of my clothes. Who eventually picked up all those clothes strung all over the house? You guessed it, my mom. That was until I was on my own and had to face the consequences of a sloppy room. That's when the realization hit, and I began to see an amazing principle. When you put something down instead of away, you have to deal with it twice. Yikes, for a professional organizer, that is a mortal sin. Why deal with it twice, when you could deal with it only once? I soon learned (the hard way) that putting it away, not down, was smart.

Here's how this works in our everyday lives:

When working on a project on your desk, quickly put it away before starting on another project. On entering the house, put your keys in the same place every day. When you bring in the mail, put it away. Use stackables for your "to do" and your "to pay" items, and so forth. Throw as much of it away as possible. In fact, place a small garbage can beside the mailbox and dump most of it there before it even enters your home. Put your folded laundry away. Put your groceries away. Put your tools away.

Putting things away brings closure to small segments of your day. By doing this, you will never have to deal with your stuff over and over. Only once.

PARADIGM #5:

"If only I had more space... If I just had a bigger house... If only I had more..."

[PARADIGM SHIFT]

"Focus on wanting what you have, not having what you want."

In my 20-plus years of organizing homes and offices across this vast country, I have never found that my clients had a lack of space or time or whatever. The real problem was that they were trying to put too much into their space or were sticking too much into their schedules. The real culprit? Coveting or hoarding.

Coveting is wanting, going, being, doing, and having more than we can maintain. It is relying on tomorrow to bring happiness that today cannot supply. Coveting focuses on the future. Coveting says I shall have this or else.

The answer to coveting? Gratitude and contentment. Gratitude and contentment focus on the present. Focus on wanting what you have, not having what you want.

The Bible says to be content with such things as you have and that godliness with contentment is great gain.

THOMAS WATSON STATES THE FOLLOWING IN HIS BOOK, "THE ART OF DIVINE CONTENTMENT":

"Contentment teaches a man how in the midst of want to abound."

"Contentment brings the heart into order."

"Contentment settles the soul."

"If God be mine, says the contented spirit, it is enough; though I have no lands or tenements, his smile makes heaven."

"A contented spirit is a silent spirit. He has not one word to say against God."

"A contented spirit is a cheerful spirit."

"A contented spirit is a thankful spirit."

Focusing on wanting what you have will free you from being discontent over not having what you want.

PARADIGM #6:

"I never have any
time for myself. Work
never seems to stop.
I haven't been in the
bathroom alone since
last February."

ADIGM SHIFT]

ep the Sabbath 'Wholly.' Take off one

ole day every week by incorporating

the concept of a Sabbath into your

schedule."

When I discovered the meaning of the Sabbath in my life, my world was turned upside down. I discovered a secret to time management. I discovered a secret to restful weeks, and I discovered that we have no reason to be burned out. The Sabbath is a lost concept to modern man, but if it were rediscovered, it would free people of so much angst and worry. I studied the Bible and read every book on the subject, and here is what I uncovered.

THE SABBATH...

1. Is a cessation of work.

You do a different set of activities on your day off than you do all through your workweek. You stop producing and enjoy the smells, joys, and sweet free time of life. You quit laboring at anything that is work for the purpose of accomplishment.

2. Is an antidote to workaholism.

The main reason that we are robbed of our Sabbath rest is busyness and the rush for more. The following is a quote from Chuck Swindoll: "Busyness, our answer to pressure, is to run faster, accomplish more. Busyness is a sign of success and importance. We attempt to impress people with a full schedule. We express aloud [our need] for relief from all we live under; but the truth is, if someone provided a way out, we wouldn't know what to do. Busyness is a way of life."

3. Provides a boundary to your week.

It brings closure to your week and gives you new energy for the following week. It enables you to return to your work with renewed vigor.

4. Says that even God rested and was refreshed.

In the Old Testament in the book of Exodus, chapter 31, verse 13, it says that God rested and was refreshed on the last day after He created the world. So, for example, if your Sabbath is Sunday, then when Monday arrives, if you feel rested and refreshed, you've experienced a Sabbath. If God took a rest, and He tells you to take a rest, then He will provide for you. God rested, He ceased work, He was a rester and a worker. You will be rested and refreshed.

5. Is a day to pray and play.

God Himself has given you approximately 49 days. That's seven and a half weeks of vacation. The Sabbath is a free day, so play. For six days you have produced. For this one day, enjoy what you have worked for.

6. Is a great time management tool.

It directly affects your following week. You are more relaxed and restored, renewed to face the new week. The Sabbath gives us extra strength and energy for the tasks of the other six days. You receive a renewed spirit, creative insights, fresh perspective.

7. Is a step of faith.

You must trust in God's sovereignty. You are not in control; God is. You can trust Him, because He controls the universe. We embrace the sovereignty of God. We don't have to struggle to work things out, because God will provide.

IN THE END, KEEPING THE SABBATH "WHOLLY" WILL BRING:

Integrity

Order

Renewed thinking

Completeness

A nurtured self

Spirit of Joy

Empowerment

Health to your Body

LET'S FACE IT...
WORK WILL NEVER STOP, SO WE MUST
STOP WORK.

PARADIGM # 7:

"I have so much
stuff, but I can't
seem to let any of
it go."

"When you buy something new,
give away two."

In my home seminars, I am constantly sharing the need for all of us to cut back, cut out, cut down, and cut away. We all have too much stuff. Think of all you have to do with your stuff once you bring it home. Here is a list of what is involved in just maintaining our possessions. You have to protect it, clean it, pay for it, worry over it, hide it, argue over it, care for it, preserve it, weigh it, ponder over it, haul it, thrash through it, brood over it, keep track of it, store it, insure it, move it, apologize for it, tend to it, guard it, collect it, hunt for it, decide about it, dig out from under it, stew over it, sort it. Polish it, buff it, wax it, strip it, prime it, oil it, dust it, water it, wash it, press it, bleach it, stretch it, dye it, scrub it, trim it, hem it, hang it, hammer it, level it, spray it, shampoo it, adjust it, wire it, glue it, sweep it, paint it, lacquer it. You are worn out with all your stuff. Once you look at what's involved in keeping so much stuff, perhaps you will be inspired to eliminate. "When you buy something new, give away two." Keep that little saying in your mind, and when you buy a new sweater or pair of shoes, give away at least two of something, maybe a shirt, pants, or old jacket. That way you will never get into the hoarding mentality, and your stuff will never control you; you will be in control of your stuff.

Think about it. Just look at the amount of stuff we bring into our offices and homes as compared to how much goes out. We focus on buying new office furniture or a new gadget, a sweater, suit, shoes, couch, table or TV, but rarely do we spend any time focused on eliminating. When was the last time we intentionally gave away two of anything when we brought a new item into our offices and homes?

Our cabinets can only hold so many dishes. Our drawers can only hold a certain number of files. When the drawer is bulging, that's a sign that we must eliminate. This is hard, because the dishes are a gift from a special friend, the files represent a major project you worked on for three years, that old rickety table brings fond memories of our college days, and on and on. We hold onto, instead of releasing.

Sharing our good fortune with those less fortunate is a freeing, liberating experience. Gathering, packing, and taking our used furniture, clothes, or whatever and offering them to the nearest Salvation Army will set you free from the hoarding mentality to enjoy simplicity at its fullest.

After all, "It is not the man who has so little who is poor. . . . It's the man who constantly craves for more."

PARADIGM #8:

"It just seems I am
constantly plagued
by little irritants
that absorb my time
and eat up my day."

"Organize your environment by removing small irritants that hinder your achievement." (Well, there goes the spouse.) ☺

I have found that when my clients move into a new office, they immediately start work and don't give themselves adequate time to set up their nests (get organized). I had a client in Colorado who hired me to give my daylong workshop and provide hands-on coaching for 12 of his people. While working with one attendee, I entered her office and, to my amazement, it was beautiful. Nothing was out of place, everything was organized, and it was gorgeous to boot. I asked the owner of the office why she took the course. She replied that there was something about the office that had been bugging her for years, and she couldn't put her finger on it.

I told her that I could not help her, that the office was close to perfect, but she insisted that I spend some time there analyzing her situation. As I watched her begin her work, the phone rang, and she reached for it. The cord was about 25 feet long, and she began to wrap it around her desk, her neck, and her computer. It was a nightmare to watch. After she hung up, I asked her if she always answered the phone like that, and she said, "Yes, and it drives me crazy." The phone was on her right, and she was right-handed, so the long cord lay across her writing area and was in the way all over her desk.

I suggested that she put the phone on her left. It took us three minutes to move the phone. It then rang. She picked it up with much ease, talked for a moment, hung up, got up, and gave me a hug. And I got big bucks for that!

She had lived with that little irritant for seven years.

Find those small easy to change irritants and get rid of them.

PARADIGM #9:

"Stuff is everywhere.
I can never find
anything."

"Assign a place for everything. Give everything a home."

Now, I know your mother told you that a hundred times when you were younger. If she was like my Mom, she pounded it into your head. And yet, it's the epitome of being organized. It is the one clear definition of what it means to have an organized environment.

So many clients are shocked when, in my seminars, I prove to them that they are more organized than they think. How do I prove it? I give them a drawer to organize, and with no rules, I just tell them they have three minutes to organize the drawer. They do it every time. How do they know how to do it? Order is naturally built into your system, your DNA, because God created you, and He put it there. After all, He is a God of order, and He embedded it into your very fiber. Somewhere along the way, it got buried, but it's there. Let me prove it to you.

Look at your knife, fork, and spoon drawer. Everyone has one, and everyone has Rubbermaid® in it. In one Rubbermaid® drawer tray, you have knives, in the other, forks, and so on. Who taught you how to do that? Why do you do that? It's intuitive. You know to do it because, as I said, it's built in. With the utensil drawer, you have actually organized that drawer using my maxim that I teach in my seminars. You have assigned your utensils a place (drawer), using containers (Rubbermaid®) that hold only one type of item (forks in one, spoons in one, and so forth). That's organization. Now repeat that same concept throughout your whole office and home. You can do it. I've seen it over and over. When you assign everything a place you will be able to find it instantly.

PARADIGM #10:

"If I don't do it, who will?"

[PARADIGM SHIFT]

"Never do for others what they can do for themselves."

"If I don't do it, who will?" I hear this well-seasoned expression in many of my seminars, especially when speaking to women. Now I know some men say it too, but we women are notorious users of the phrase, and we live it.

My mother, the mother of nurturers, epitomized this maxim. She often told me that she had to think for herself, my dad, and me for years. Now, were we lazy? Yes. Were we irresponsible? Yes. However, I think my mom brought this on herself when she did for us what we really could have done for ourselves.

This sort of scenario repeated itself many times when I was growing up: My mom, dad, and I worked side by side in our country grocery store serving the farmers as they worked the land. Mom would occasionally holler from the store for me to find a wrench or whatever she might need at the time. I would begrudgingly search for the wrench, but I also knew how to work it so my mom would have to end up getting the wrench herself. I would hunt through the drawer in the kitchen and then yell that I couldn't find the wrench. She would then shout back that it was in the drawer next to the stove. I would make a lot of noise as I rummaged through the drawer and then go tell her that I couldn't find the wrench. By then she was frustrated and would throw up her hands, go into the kitchen, promptly march to the drawer, open it, and—voilà!—there was the wrench in plain view. Imagine that!

I won the battle. After several sessions, I had trained my mom not to ask me to find her anything. Mom would always give in and do the project herself, and I won the battle. But I lost the war and the character development that would have transpired if she had hung in there and required that I find the wrench.

When it came to my 4-H projects, she made me do the projects but for smaller things like look for a wrench, she did it for me.

Never, never do for others what they can do for themselves. This is not a set-in-cement maxim, but more often than not, it's a better philosophy to live by than "If I don't do it, who will?"

PARADIGM #11:

"Organization just
doesn't work for me.
I straighten up my
office many times,
but it just doesn't
stay."

[PARADIGM SHIFT]
"Organization is not straightening,
neatening, or rearranging. Organization
is establishing a system."

The key word here is "straighten." If you straightened, you didn't organize, and that's why it easily became chaotic again.

So many of my clients let things pile up for months. Then, once they are sufficiently frustrated with the mess, they come in on a Saturday and spend the whole day cleaning up. The trouble is, they straightened, or tidied. That's not organizing.

If you straighten, tidy, or clean without establishing a system, your office or home will soon fall back into disorganization. Read on to discover my system and my five-step process for decluttering and restoring order to your office and home.

PARADIGM #12:

"I don't know where to start."

[PARADIGM SHIFT]
"Think S.T.A.R.T. Start today an action to reach your target."

For many of my clients, saying that they don't know where to start is a guaranteed action stopper. Because they don't know where to start, and it's all so overwhelming, they immediately give up without even trying. Let's start with changing our thinking.

Think S.T.A.R.T.

Start Today an Action to Reach your Target. You start with my simple five-step procedure for organizing just about everything you own.

1) Remove
2) Sort
3) Eliminate
4) Contain
5) Assign

I will explain these five steps in detail a bit later in the book.

PARADIGM #13:

"I have so much to do, I will never get it all done."

"Divide and conquer. Remember, home (and office) weren't built in a day."

You've heard the saying "By the yard, it's hard, but by the inch, it's a cinch"? It's true. Instead of looking at the whole, look at each part and think divide and conquer. Break it up into bite-size steps. Now I know you do this all the time. When you are cooking lasagna, you brown the meat while the noodles are cooking. As you are cooking the sauce, you add spices, and so on. You don't throw all these ingredients in the pot at once; you divide and conquer by doing one step at a time. It's the same principle with whatever project you are working on. Divide into achievable small steps, conquer each step, and the project is finished.

I learned about the principles of order through 4-H while in grade school and high school. I was involved up to my neck in 4-H projects, traipsing the forests for insects and larvae, refinishing furniture, sewing formals, and hooking rugs. I had from September until July to finish each project. How did I accomplish such daunting tasks? By my mom's constant prodding and by "divide and conquer." One small step for me, one finished project for the 4-H fair. Every detail had to be planned and thought through; supplies had to be bought, goals established, time scheduled.

It required persistent work, day after day. Plod on, plod on. By working 30 minutes to one hour every day, in the end, I had gorgeous dresses, refinished furniture, and a beautiful collection of insects (four cases still hang on my wall; Smithsonian, eat your heart out). I accomplished all these projects by dividing and conquering.

PARADIGM #14:

"If I can just get these little jobs out of the way, I'll have the time to focus on what's really important."

"Do the most important project at the beginning of the day." (Your life fits around your top priorities.)

Tell me truthfully, will we ever have the time to focus on what's really important? Probably not. We must make the time to focus on what is really important. Writing this book is an example. When I focused in the early morning on writing one chapter at a time, I usually got it done, and then everything else also got accomplished. When I had tried to get rid of the small, quick projects hanging over my head first, I never had the time to write.

When are you at your freshest? For most of us, it's 6 to 12 o'clock in the morning. Now some of you are night owls, or your energy level skyrockets at midday. But most people have told me that their shutters bang in the early part of their day. That's when you should do the most important project. That report that needs finishing—tackle it at 7:30 before anyone else comes to the office. The planning that's needed to remodel your kitchen—do it before the kids wake up or right after they've gone to school. Work steadily for one hour on your most important task, and the hardest is over. You've put your best energy, sharpest thinking on the most important project. Everything for the rest of the day will be downhill.

PARADIGM #15:

"I need a large clump of time to start a project. It's all or nothing with me. If I can't find three hours for this project, I'll never get it done."

"Break large projects into smaller time segments, doable throughout the day, to reduce idle time."

Many of us will never have large clumps of time to work on a project. Life is too full of people and events. Kids, extended family, places to go, things to do, coworkers, phones, faxes, e-mails, voice mail. We could never find consistently an hour here and there to work on a project. That's why it's important to take each project (goal) and break it into 15-minute segments. In a project notebook, write out all the small steps involved in your project and plan them, 15 minutes at a time, into your day.

Here's the beauty of this principle. When you find that occasionally during your day, you have found 15 minutes of lag time, you then go to your project notebook and find a goal that you can work on for 15 minutes. Voilà! You have filled the 15-minute slot, not with wandering around doing nothing, but with a project that needs to be done.

PARADIGM #16:

"I just don't have enough time."

[PARADIGM SHIFT]
"You have all the time there is."

Take a few minutes and look at your office. Are you thinking from a misplaced paradigm? Are you thinking, "I don't have enough time"? If so, look at that statement from another perspective and begin to realize that you have all the time there is. When you see time from that perspective, it changes everything, and you begin managing your time based on another paradigm. All of a sudden, time takes on a whole new meaning, which in turn affects how you spend your time and handle your schedule.

Time management is a misnomer. You can't manage time. You can only manage the events of your life or your priorities. You can't save time or enhance time; you can't buy it, sell it, store it, loan it, multiply it, change it, manufacture it, or rent it.

You can only spend time. Realize that you have all the time you need to accomplish what God created you to accomplish. After all, He's the creator of you and your day. He not only orchestrates the dance of the planets, the stars, and the cosmos, but He is intricately interested in your every day. He is the originator of time, and He can guide you best in the most productive use of your time.

As you respond to His timetable, projects begin to get done in record time. Why? Because you are doing His projects His way, not just doing activities that produce nothing.

PARADIGM #17:

"If I file it, I will
never find it. Out of
sight, out of mind."

"It's not the filing you fear, nor is it the out-of-sight, out-of-mind; it's the lack of a system."

When people say they fear they'll forget their files if they put them away, I tell them that it's not filing they fear; it's their filing system. Let me prove this point to you by asking you some questions. Do you have all your pots and pans out all over your floor in your kitchen? Do you have all your underwear and socks and T-shirts out all over your bedroom? Do you have all your bath towels out all over your hallway? I am sure that your answers to all these questions are no, of course not. Well, why not? How can you possibly find your pans, underwear, socks or T-shirts if you don't have them out where you can see them?

Do you see how ridiculous it would be if you had everything lying out so you wouldn't forget where you put them? So why do you need your files out in front of you? You don't. It's just that you fear your filing system. You can find your pans, underwear, socks and towels because you have taken a minute to assign them a place, and you have put them in a certain container (cabinet, drawer, and so on). So do the same for your files. Take some time to decide on a filing system that works for you. Once you have thought through your filing system and set it up, filing will be a breeze. Never again will you need all your files piled all over your floor so you know where they are. Your filing system will be so simple that it will actually encourage you to file into it. I will explain my snappy FileMAP® System a little later in the book.

PARADIGM #18:

"When I was growing up, I had so little that I want my kids never to experience the poverty that I went through."

"Focus on giving your kids what you have, instead of focusing on providing them with what you didn't have."

You know what I have discovered while working with families all over this great country as I organize their homes and offices? Almost everywhere I go, I see moms and dads struggling and muddling through mountains of toys that they have worked to supply their kids with, and few kids appreciate it. Parents think that if they don't get their kids all these toys, educational games, and computer programs, they are depriving them of much needed intelligence.

Here's a novel idea. Instead of giving your kids something that is perishable and will just add to the junk heap in some landfill, try giving them the following: Take them to the zoo; start taking them on walks in the park; get them off the computer and out into nature; teach them how to serve by requiring them to take a few hours each month and visit a hospital or work with Habitat For Humanity®; start having just plain good family time once a week at home without turning on the TV. Sit around the fireplace and begin developing family rituals that they will remember for years to come. You can find all kinds of things to do with your kids that are free. I've just given you a few ideas to spur your imagination. More than anything that my dad bought for me, all I wanted when I was growing up was for him to come out and play ball with me and the neighborhood kids. That's all I remember that I wanted.

PARADIGM #19:

"But if I clear off
my desk, it will
look like I don't
have any work."

[PARADIGM SHIFT]
"A cleared desk is a sign of efficiency and effectiveness."

In my seminars, every time I show a before and after picture of an office that I have organized, some of the attendees comment that the after picture looks like the guy doesn't have any work to do. I share with them that their thought about the after picture is actually their paradigm or mindset about an organized desk. I tell them that to organize their lives, they will have to begin changing their thinking as well as their offices and homes. Of course this whole book is about changing your thinking about order and your concept of what order is and is not. You must begin to see that a cleared-off counter in your home or an empty desktop does not signify that you do little or no work.

Have we ever once thought when we see a completely cleared desk at our work site that, just maybe, that person is efficient or effective? We usually think just the opposite. I once worked with a client who told me that a cluttered desk was a sign that he was busy and important to his company. He equated clutter on top of his desk with busyness, which translated to "I will keep my job because I am a busy man."

Start thinking that putting things away is a sign of organization and competency. Begin thinking that orderliness is next to godliness, and you will begin to make changes in your environment as well.

PARADIGM #20:

"Getting organized
will constrain me
or confine me."

[PARADIGM SHIFT]
"Real order liberates."

I once had a roommate from California. She was a neat gal with many talents, and I cared for her as a friend. Being from California, she was very hip and fun-loving. She loved parties and was the life of every one she went to. While I moved over to the side of the room and had a deep conversation with just one of the party attendees, she covered the whole room. Flitting like a butterfly from one person to another, she thrived on meeting everyone she could. She once told me that she didn't want to be organized, because she felt that getting organized would constrain her and tie her down.

I, of course, told her that it did just the opposite. It liberates. When you are organized, you can go to the party and not feel guilty that the dishes are not done and that you will have to face them when you get home. When you are organized, you have more time to spend with loved ones. When you are organized, you have more time, so you can enjoy when people drop by or attend a party. You are not constantly thinking about your chores left undone.

Order liberates, and as Jack Welch, past CEO of General Electric, once said, "Eliminating clutter allows faster decision-making."

PARADIGM #21:

"Getting organized doesn't help, cause I will never stay organized. I will just mess it up, and it will fall back into chaos."

[PARADIGM SHIFT]

"Once you are organized, spend only one minute per hour of every day maintaining the organization."

Here's another shocking paradigm. I share in my seminars that after you have organized your office or home, it will only take you one minute of every hour to maintain the order. That's right, spend only one minute every hour maintaining that order and you will never be disorganized again. People seem to think that getting organized takes a monumental amount of time, but that staying organized takes even more time. This is not true. Maintaining your organization is really quite easy once your paradigm has been shifted. Remember to allot one minute per hour for the upkeep, and you will be organized forever.

Organizing is investing the time on the front end to reap the time on the back end. Whatever time you spend organizing and maintaining that order, you will get all of that time back! Is that fabulous, or what?

I hope you have enjoyed these ideas and paradigms. As you begin the process of changing your thought patterns, you will reap the benefits everyday.

If you get a chance, let me know how these ideas have helped you. I would love to hear from you. God bless you in your endeavor to organize your thinking.

PART II

How to Organize Your Office

OVERVIEW

"Lady, I need your help. I read about you in the Washington Post and I think you can help me de-clutter my desk. I'm an editor of a paper in the D.C. area and I have mounds of paper all over my efficiency apartment. Can you organize all my files and papers at my home?"

This man sounded desperate, so I responded cheerfully, "Yes, I'll be there first thing next Monday." Little did I know what I was about to face. Fresh and excited about the possibility of working with an editor, I bounced out of bed and planned my strategy to attack his papers.

He lived in an efficiency apartment in Northwest D.C. and as I entered, I was hit in the face with dust balls—yes dust balls—stalactites hanging from the ceiling, dust balls waving in the air-conditioning, like streamers at a party. As I slid across the floor on a three-inch layer of dust, I marveled, "Why is your apartment so dusty?"

"Well, I travel sometimes nine months at a time out of the country and all I do is work."

I laughed nervously and said, "This dust looks like it's been here longer than nine months. When was the last time you cleaned your apartment?"

"1981" was the reply. This was 1997.

I looked around and noticed that there were a few loose papers lying around, but not very many. He led me to the kitchen, which was picked up and clean, but he had hidden in every cabinet, tons of papers stuffed where the dishes usually reside. There was not one plate, pan, glass or utensil in his kitchen, and no food.

"Where do you eat?" I asked.

"I've eaten out for the past 15 years," was his reply.

Many people are literally buried by paperwork at their office or in their homes, and few know where to start to excavate their desk and find a workable solution to all those pieces of paper lying around.

A cluttered desk is a waste of time. It is not only distracting, but draining. You can't possibly be excited about going to the office if you are knee-deep in paperwork. Hundreds of executives, managers and secretaries I have worked with have been set free with a simple desk system that eliminates clutter and offers them a concrete way to organize their files, papers, computer files, e-mails and supplies.

WHAT ORGANIZATION IS NOT

One of the first questions I ask in my seminars across the country is, "Have you ever organized a drawer in your office and in a few days it returned to its original chaos?" The answers come in waves of mumblings and agonizing groans. Yes is the resounding response. It happens all the time. They then tell me they regressed because they lack discipline, or don't take the time to maintain, or their spouses mess things up, and so on. I then give them immediate hope by saying the reason the drawer slipped back is not because of lack of discipline but because they did not organize in the first place. They did something else and called it organizing.

Frequently someone will tell me how he or she came into their office over a Saturday, eliminated massive amounts of clutter and felt quite good about the accomplishment, but shortly thereafter, it slipped back. They didn't organize, they did something else. Let's look at what they did and **therefore define what organizing is NOT.**

Organizing is not REARRANGING.

Many of my clients rearrange or straighten their stuff. If they do that, the chaos will return.

Organizing is not TIDYING OR CLEANING.

Most of us spend way too much time cleaning. It's not the dirt that makes you nervous, it's the clutter. Stop Cleaning!!! (I get standing ovations for this idea). Spend more time on organizing and less time on cleaning. You'll love me for this tip.

Organizing is not HIDING.

Your boss comes through and tells you the Board of Directors are coming today. What do most of us do? We quickly open our drawers or cabinets and hide all our stuff out of sight!

Organizing is not PERFECTIONISM.

You do not have to have your hangers arranged one inch apart in your closet in order to be organized.

Organization is not NATURAL.

One of my clients at 3M™ raised his hand and said "Organizing is not natural!" Another client said, "Lady, for me it's not possible!"

Organization is not a MORAL ISSUE.

You don't need to feel guilty if you are not organized.

Organization is not the SAME FOR EVERYONE.

There is no set way to organize anything. It's based on your personality and the amount of stuff you own and the amount of space that you have. Isn't that good? Does that make you feel better already? For years you have rearranged, straightened, neatened, hid, or cleaned. No longer. From now on you will correctly organize. Let's look at the true meanings of organizing.

WHAT ORGANIZATION IS

Winnie-the-Pooh said it succinctly, "Organizing is what you do before you do it, so that when you do it, it's not all mixed up."

If you were an organized person in most aspects of your life, what would you look like, how would you live out your everyday life?

IN YOUR ENVIRONMENT, YOU WOULD:

Assign special areas for all your possessions.

Give every article, item, supply, and file a place and a home. We will talk about this idea a bit later.

Prepare yourself and your environment for its greatest efficiency.

Ever observe a dentist as he works his magic in your mouth? Rarely does the guy ever move from one spot. He can reach any tool in one motion in seconds. That's how you want your office to run, reaching any item, article, supply, file, or book in one motion.

Take care of what you own to extend its usefulness.

Stewardship is the word. It's a biblical term, but has wide ramifications. We do not own anything. We can take nothing with us when we die. We can only steward what God has given us. Everything we have is derived.

Remove obstacles that hinder your achievement.

I worked with a manager at Marriott® several years ago. Every morning he would enter his office, unlock his desk and all his drawers would fall open. Whenever he needed to take a break or leave the office he would have to rear back in his seat, place both feet on all drawers at the same time, and reach over and lock his desk. I mentioned that all we needed to do was call a maintenance man to fix the problem-a problem that had plagued him for 7 years! We have little obstacles or irritants in our offices that plague us, rob us of our time and energy.

Simplify your lifestyle by sharing with others.

I mention this idea in my seminars all across the country. I usually get blank stares. Some people have so little. Many of us have plenty. Why not share from our good fortune? Begin the process of getting rid of the old by passing it down to less fortunate people.

> Being ORGANIZED IN YOUR ENVIRONMENT means being able to find and easily get to what you own.

IN YOUR WORK HABITS, YOU WOULD:

Sharpen your axe.

Reminds me of a story. There was this woodsman who was hired to cut down trees. He was paid by the tree. So early Monday morning, energized and excited, he cut down 20 trees! The next day, rearing to go, he cut down another 20 trees. Wednesday, he once again rose early and began the process, but this day he cut down only 10 trees. Thursday he cut down 5 trees, and Friday it looked like he was going to cut down 5. What was his problem?

Most people in my seminars don't get the right answer. They suggest that all the trees are gone, or the other trees are in his way, or he has lost energy, he is tired, or whatever. Rarely do they guess the real reason- his axe is dull. In order to return to cutting down 20 trees, he must take the time to sharpen his axe. But to sharpen his axe, he must stop his producing and maintain good equipment. The problem is, he says, that he doesn't have time, so he continues to work with a dull axe and continues to cut down only 5 trees a day. Organizing is investing the time on the front end to reap the time on the back end.

Do right things as well as do things right.

We are notorious at spending time on the peripheral. We know how to do things right, but spend most of our time majoring on the minors. You've heard the saying, "Efficiency is doing things right, effectiveness is doing right things." It's true.

Know your limitation, by recognizing co-workers' and spouse's strengths.

This is a hard one. Many of us, especially women, tend to do it all ourselves. We are like the Statue of Liberty in the New York Harbor. She stands with outstretched arms saying "Give me your tired, your poor." We find ourselves doing too much and we do tasks that we are not well equipped to do. Consequently, we don't give the people who are gifted in those areas a chance to operate in their strengths. We end up operating in our weaknesses, and we get burned out.

Develop standards, fences and boundaries.

This is another hard one. In order to accomplish more and become better organized, we must become more in control. Developing standards, especially for our schedules, will lend itself to less stress, more control, less confusion, and more time. What do I mean by developing standards or boundaries? Take the example of supper. Most American families have lost the art of having a relaxed supper with the full family. It has disappeared from the American landscape. It is a strong tool to bind and hold families together, yet we have succumbed to soccer, ballet, and whatever, and have relegated family supper to the ash heap. Let's set some boundaries. Let's begin to say enough is enough. Let's take back our families. Let's take back the quiet, peaceful time of gathering around the supper table for food, fun and fellowship. Let's set some guidelines and boundaries and then stick to them.

Be content with your present lifestyle.

I have found that one of the reasons it is so hard to get organized is that we are discontent. Our society teaches it, the TV applauds it, our nature revels in it. We are a nation of discontent. The more content you are with your environment and your stuff, the easier it is to get organized.

Reject distractions that hinder you
from reaching your goals.

Again, we are a nation of distractions. We love to
have it this way. When we are torn in a million pieces,
we cannot concentrate on anything effectively.

> Being ORGANIZED IN YOUR
> WORK HABITS means you will
> be more productive in your
> workday

IN YOUR SPIRIT, YOU WOULD:

Respond to your season in life.

This simply means that we all have seasons that we go
through. Knowing what your season is and embracing
it is key to staying organized. For instance, if you are
a young mother and work full time in a job, it would
not be wise to try to start a new business. Embrace
your season of Motherhood and working full time as
enough to attain at one time. Trying to do too much
by resisting your season can be devastating.

Guard diligently your priorities.

Priorities are the stuff of life. They are what give
your life focus and meaning. Without knowing and
guarding our priorities, we will flounder, flop and fly

in all directions. Recognizing, establishing, planning, living out your priorities will add direction, purpose, solidification to our schedules, lives and spirits.

Know your purpose in life.

Purpose is that inner depth in our heart and soul where we have an intuitive sense of who we are, where we came from, and where we are going. Our lives are divinely ordained and significant. We are not an accident! God made us with a history and a story that nobody else has. He put us in a distinctive time and place in history—we are one of a kind. Having purpose means that something motivates us to action. When we focus on that action, it orders our schedule and draws us closer to God.

> Being ORGANIZED IN YOUR SPIRIT means being able to live in a consistent rest and contentment

THE BENEFITS OF GETTING ORGANIZED

Now that we have discussed the definition of organizing, let's look at the benefits. The practical benefits are easy to see.

space	You will gain 25-40% more space in your file cabinets, desk drawers, shelves and storage areas.
time	You will gain ½ -1 hour of time each day simply because you are no longer going through your work to get to your work. No longer hunting for your work, it will be accessible and easy to find.
energy	You get instant energy once your desk and office are organized.
control	Organizing any area of your life brings better control over the place, priorities and people that you deal with on a daily basis.
money	The bottom line, you will save and make your company money, and you will find your company money. I found a real-estate agent $2,000, a man in VA, a table saw (with the table), Marriott® in North Carolina $1200, and a woman in Maryland, $30,000.

Those listed above are just a few of the benefits you will experience as you begin the process of organizing.

WHAT ARE SOME OF THE SIGNS OF AND REASONS FOR CHAOS AND CLUTTER?

What are we experiencing on a daily basis that should tell us that we are disorganized and that we need to address this problem?

- Some of us hold onto too much of our old stuff, or have to hunt for our files.
- Some lose time looking for paperwork or are easily distracted.
- We fail to finish projects on time or miss important deadlines.
- Some have multiple filing systems or paperwork strewn everywhere.
- Some of my clients think that the above situations are not problems at all. It is the way they normally live. They don't recognize that they are disorganized. So I have developed a statement that will immediately tell you if you are disorganized and need to stop work and set up a system.

Here's the statement; **Do you go through your work to get to your work?**

Once you ask yourself that question, you will know which areas of your office need to be changed.

WHAT IS THE COST OF CLUTTER?

What is disorganization costing you? Take this test.
Fill in the blanks:

	Example	Your Company
Minutes per day wasted looking for files	A 30 minutes	A _____
Avg. annual salary ($30,000) divided by 1000	B $30	B _____
Divide B by 2	C $15	C _____
Divide C by 60	D $0.25	D _____
Multiply A times D times 220	E $1650	E _____
Multiply E times the number of people (50) in your company	F $82,500	F _____

This chart quickly informs you of the tremendous waste and cost of corporate and personal clutter. Eliminating clutter and establishing a system will set you on the road to achieving more in less time, there will be less stress and more time for you to do what matters most.

PURPOSE OR MEANING OF ORDER

Now let's look at why we need to get organized. If you can't answer that question, when you begin the process and are lost in your clutter, you will soon be overwhelmed and will stop the process because it will be too massive to finish. You must answer the question, why?

And here is the main reason I feel that you need to be more organized:

> Simplicity is where we are headed. Organizing will simplify your life to allow you to focus more on what matters most to you and focus less on what does not matter.

You will more easily discover your purpose in life and begin doing what you do best more effectively. Whether you are an individual or a corporation, once you are more organized, you will be able to focus on what matters most. That is concentration, that is focus, that will lend itself to you getting more done in less time thus becoming more productive and focusing on what really counts for you. That could be work shorter hours or it could be spend quality time with your family. Whatever you want to do, organizing will allow you to do it more effectively.

THE FIVE STEPS TO A MORE ORGANIZED YOU

If you were to organize your lap drawer in your desk (the middle drawer that is over your knees), where would you start? I ask that question in every seminar I give across the country and invariably people say they take it all out and throw away what they don't need. Some may group items together, and then they put it all back. This is not organizing, it is simply rearranging, and that is why it soon returns to chaos. I am finding that the main reason people are not organized is because they've never been trained. Business

> The main reason people are not organized is because they have never been trained.

schools train managers to manage people but not how to manage their desks. Secretarial schools teach secretaries how to type 140 words per minute, but no clue is offered as to how to organize their desks.

Let me share with you five simple steps to a more organized you. These five steps will be woven throughout this entire section, but first let's look at them directly.

Perhaps this picture looks like your desk drawer.

1) REMOVE

Suppose you were going to organize your lap drawer. What would be the first step you would have to do? One woman in my seminar shouted, "I'd close the drawer and go have a sweet roll!" One man said, "I can't get my drawer open." Whatever your situation may be, the very first step would be to remove all the stuff—take out all the pens, pencils, clips, rubber bands, twist ties, packages of sugar, tea bags, McDonald's™ mustard and ketchup packets, business cards, loose papers, 3x5 cards, photos, keys, Post-it® notes, dried up sandwiches, caked on candy, toothbrushes. Whatever lurks in the deep recesses of the drawer, take it out. It probably hasn't seen light in seven years—it needs a breath of fresh air.

2) SORT

As you are removing all items, sort according to like items. Most people just take it all out and pile it on the top of the desk or on the floor. It's hard to see what you have if you do it that way. Sorting like items will clue you to the fact that you have 87 pens and 830 clips. You might ask yourself, "Do I need so many?" Also sorting helps you to ...

3) ELIMINATE

After you have sorted and you see that many of your pens are dried up or that the sugar packages have mated and grown exponentially, you can eliminate. You either throw them directly into the trash or you have a box labeled **to go elsewhere**. Into that box goes any item that does not belong in your office. After you have finished the drawer, take the **go elsewhere** box and distribute the stuff to where it goes, perhaps back into the office supply cabinet.

4) CONTAIN

Now comes the most fabulous step, the one most people leave out. For those of you who have gotten this far, stop and think. If you just put all these groups of pens, pencils, ruler, stamps, and clips back in the drawer, in a few short days they will be a jumbled mess again. How do you keep those groups sorted and separated at all

times? By first containing them. Put each group in a container, a drawer divider, or a shallow box before you place them back in the drawer, they will stay contained and not fly all over the drawer again.

5) ASSIGN

This step is the key. Don't just stick the containers in the drawer. Assign them a place. Anytime you say the word **stick-it** ("I'll just stick it here" or "I'll just put it in here for now" or "I'll just lay it here until I need it") you have just created clutter! Don't put things down, put them away. However, to put them away, you must assign them a place. How do you know where to put things if you have never assigned them a place? You may put them here one day or there the next. The items have a tendency to float from place to place. Assign those containers a defined place in the drawer.

　　You have done it! These are the fabulous five steps that we will be using all throughout the rest of this book. Now let's take a look at what an office, its desk and files, etc. are supposed to look like.

THE DESK

There are all sorts of desks, all shapes and sizes, and there are many types of offices, small, oblong and large. I'm not going to be able to draw your office but I can tell you the ideal desk and equipment to buy. You can arrange your bookshelf and computer accordingly.

How should an office look and what should it offer? I firmly believe you need a minimum of four file drawers, four small drawers in or near your desk and one bookshelf. If you have two saw horses and a door for a desk, somewhere near it you need a minimum of four file drawers and four small drawers and one bookshelf.

Now that you have a list of furniture that you need for your office, let's start by defining each item in your office and giving it a place. Believe it or not, you only have four major items in your office (other than your computer):

- Files
- Small supplies that go into your desk drawers
- Loose papers
- Books/resources and larger supplies that go on shelves

FILES USING THE FILEMAP® SYSTEM

If you stop to analyze your files, you'll see that you've done the same thing with your files that you did with your clothes closet in your home. You stuffed all your files into one or two drawers and they're all crammed in and you can't even get to them much less find them. The secret to organizing your files is to set them up according to how often you use them and place the most

> Set your files up according to how often you use them.

often used nearest you. In your office you have at least three types of files.

THE FILEMAP® SYSTEM

MAIN. These are the files that you are now working on, they are actively a part of your job. You may be working on one project, your budget, and three personal files. These current working files go in your Main drawer.

ARCHIVE. All other files that do not fit in your Main drawer, go into your Archive drawers. These files are the ones you've not looked at for 13 years, no one else has looked at them, you've never used them, you're not going to use them, but you might need them some day.

PERSONAL. This drawer contains all your personal files, like your insurance papers, your pay stubs, or your 401K or evaluations. Some of my clients use this file drawer to house their purse or jogging shoes.

For those of you who have a home office, you would not need the Personal Drawer-all of your files at home are personal. If you like the FileMAP® concept, you could designate the "P" to be Projects if you have them or People (kids, parents, etc.)

Now within the FileMAP® System you can set up categories based on your work processes. Ask yourself what do I do, what are my work processes, what is my job function? Your work processes or job function will define your file categories. In other words, perhaps you work with clients. If so, then one of your categories is Clients. Perhaps you are in the Human Resources department and you work with compensation or benefits or recruiting. Those are your work processes and thus your file categories.

So for example you set up your 3-inch plastic file tab that reads Clients and then file your client files behind the 3-inch plastic file tab—each file represents each client. Within each file are memos, letters, invoices, whatever transactions have transpired between you and your client. On the computer your categories will mirror your paper file categories. If you are in the HR Department, the 3-inch tab will read Compensation or Benefits, and behind each tab you will file all the benefit or compensation files.

The beauty of the FileMAP® System is that as you are finishing work on a file in your Main drawer you move it to the Archive drawer. Or as you need a file that is in the Archive drawer, you move it to the **Main** drawer until you are finished with it, then it goes back into the **Archive** drawer.

Here is an example of a Human Resources Department FileMAP®:

POLICY
Chapters
Guidelines
Development
Memos

EMPLOYEE RELATIONS
Terminations
RIF
Disciplinary Action
Trustees

RECORDS
Unemployment
Memos to Record
    Employment Verification
    Change in Status
    Salary
    Leave
Correspondence Benefits
RSR
APC
In-processing

RECRUITING
Advertising
Exit Interview
Reporting
    Budget
    Monthly Report
    Interview
    Offer Accept/Decline
Relocation
Interns
College Recruiting
Trustees
Hire Awards
Drug Testing

BENEFITS
Budget
Health
Retirement
Retirees
Trustees
Leave
Compliance
Labels
Cobra
Worker Compensation
Education Assistance

COMPENSATION
Performance Review
Survey
Analyses
    Internal Equity
    Market
    New Hire
Performance Development

CORPORATE PROGRAMS
Awards
    Service Pins
    Excellence
    Joe Platt
    Quick Cash
Suggestion System
Training and Development
Associate Program
Mentor Protégé
Corporate Teams
    Casual Attire
    Recognition Design
    TFT
Trustees
Orientation

SUPPLIES

Before we talk about where the supplies go in your desk, you need to know what supplies are necessary to manage an office effectively. Below is a complete list of supplies that you may need.

File Cabinet	Pencil Sharpener
Clips	Pens
Computer/Printer	Markers
Copier	Postage Scale
Dictionary/Thesaurus	Postcards
Stackable Trays	Post-it® Notes
Drawer Dividers	Rubber Bands
Fax Machine	Scissors
File Folders	Small Baskets/Boxes for Supplies
Glue	Stamps
Labels	Stapler/Staple Remover
Labels (Pre-Addressed)	Staples
Mailing Envelopes	Stationery
Notebook	Tape and Dispenser
Pads	Telephone
Paper	Trash Can
Pencils	White-Out Fluid

Below are pictures of the most important organizers you need to effectively organize your office.

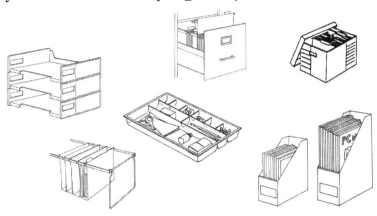

Here's where the fun begins. You wouldn't believe all the stuff I have pulled out of small drawers. One wonders how someone can get so much into these small areas. The same secret you used with your file drawer, you can use with your small drawers. Only one

> Some of my clients' offices have been affectionately called the Black Hole; they went in there last month and they're still missing. ☺

subject goes into one drawer. For example, one drawer gets pads, one drawer houses phone books, one drawer stationery, etc.

The only time you mix subjects is when you have either a divider in a small drawer or you are using containers and you can keep all utensils or items separated. These small drawers are for all your supplies. You can place any supplies too large for drawers in containers on shelving. Refer to "The Five Steps to a More Organized You" for the steps to follow to organize your small supply drawers.

LOOSE PAPERS

"Now where did I put that piece of paper? I know it's here somewhere." Sound familiar? Loose papers are

blocking out light and air and completely swamping every window sill or any horizontal surface in our offices. Some of my clients' offices have been affectionately called the

Black Hole, they went in there last month and they're still missing (just kidding).

There are two ways you can organize your papers. I will offer both ideas, you can choose which best suits your needs.

The first way to organize your avalanche of loose papers is to use my simple, snappy, succinct 3D Process using stackables:

1) Do Now   2) Do Later   3) Delegate

Do Now is **this week**—all papers you know you will have to do this week go into that stackable.

Do Later is **this month**—You need to do this, but it probably won't get done this week but needs to be looked at this month.

Delegate is **this person**—Whomever you consistently delegate work to needs a stackable. The delegate stackable can also hold papers that you need to discuss with your co-workers.

This is a very simple system that you can use especially if you have a small to medium amount of loose papers on your desk. For those of you who have to mount an expedition to find your desk because of the mountains of paperwork, you can use the same system but expand it. This is the **3D Expanded Process:**

Do Now	Do Later	Delegate
To Pay	To Read	Sam
To Call	To File	Susie
Pending	To Copy	Pete

In other words, the **Do Now, Do Later, Delegate** stackables are not enough division for you - you need more stackables than just the three. You have several types of **Do Now** and you need to subdivide them or you delegate to three people and you want all those papers to go into their individual stackable, not just piled into one stackable.

These categories are based on the action you will be taking on each of these pieces of paper. We will discuss later where we will put these stacks once we've made them.

Let's review each of these categories:

DO NOW–This stack consists of papers you will need to work on this week. It includes projects, reports, or memos you must complete this week. These are papers not files.

DO LATER–For projects or reports that are due next month.

DELEGATE/SECRETARY–If you have a secretary and you are constantly giving her work, then there will be a stack of papers somewhere on your desk that will need to get to her quickly. If you delegate to other co-workers, each of them need their own stackable.

TO READ–Most people's **to read** extends to the ceiling. One dentist I worked with had stacks of magazines in his office. He will never read these, but just in case he has the time, he's kept them handy. There's too much information coming into

> Most people's "to read" extends to the ceiling.

your office. You cannot read it all so you need to face the fact and weed out all those articles, magazines, newsletters, and newspapers. Just think of the money you'll be saving, not to mention the environment. Paper comes from trees. Trees grow slowly. Prioritize and decide what three subjects you are interested in and stop your subscriptions to all other magazines and journals. Make a **to read** stack of critical reading only.

TO PAY–Every bill you receive should go in a to **pay stack.** Mixing your bills with **your to do's** will complicate matters and you may lose track of paying an important bill. One client put his parking ticket in with the rest of his **to do's** and it grew from $35.00 to $140.00.

TO CALL–All those pink slips, messages that are scattered all over your desk and in your briefcase, need to go into a small **to call** box on your desk. If you have papers on your desk, and the next action is to make a phone call, then place these in the **to call** stackable.

TO FILE—The rest of the papers that require no action but need to be saved, go into a **to file** stackable. These will be filed in your filing cabinet.

IN-BOX–An in-box is not your **to do** box. An in-box is for papers **that you have received, but have not**

opened nor looked at. Once you open a piece of mail, or touch a piece of paper in your in-box, you must not drop it back in your in-box. It must go into one of the other stacks or files in your file drawers.

OUT-BOX–This box is for paper that you will take out of your office or will go to someone else on your staff. This out-box can be your delegate box if you wish.

Now we have analyzed and defined the type of papers we deal with on a daily basis. We've defined all the supplies in your small drawers and we have defined your files. We are left now with...

BOOKS, RESOURCES AND LARGER SUPPLIES

The best way to organize books, magazines, resources and large supplies is to use bookshelves and plenty of them. Place books together and put magazines in magazine cardboard holders. Computer books, CD's, etc. can be stored together on the shelving. Letterhead stationery, Xerox® paper can go into stackables and extra supplies all go into containers on the shelving.

We have just described what your equipment should look like and how your files, supplies and loose papers,

and books/resources should be categorized. Now let's actually do the step-by-step organizing.

THE ORGANIZING APPROACH

Let's review the five steps.
1)   Remove
2)   Sort
3)   Eliminate
4)   Contain
5)   Assign

ORGANIZE YOUR FILES!

Where do we start? Well, you start by creating space and to create space you have to empty your file drawers. Start with your file drawer in your desk. The drawer you want your Main working files to go into. Remove each file and sort it on the floor into one of the categories defined earlier.

MAIN–those files you are now working on
ARCHIVE–dead files
PERSONAL–your own personal files

Choose just one drawer and literally **1) remove** and **2) sort** every file that is presently in that file drawer. When you finish you will have a small Main stack, a huge Archive stack and a medium Personal stack. Now **3) eliminate** the files you don't need and purge from the files the duplicated or unwanted papers. There is no sense in keeping papers that you will never need. Next **4) contain** these files by **5) assigning** the Main files back into the desk drawer you just emptied. The other two stacks **(Archive and Personal)** will be placed in your other file drawers once they are emptied. Go to the next drawer and repeat the steps above. The files you use a lot will be in your Main drawer nearest you. The files you use least will be farther away in the Archive drawers. If you only have one or two drawers total, you can combine two categories in one drawer only if you keep them completely separated. Also, file each file alphabetically within its own category. Now what have you done? You have created a beautiful filing system in which all those loose files and papers that are now lying all around your office can be filed. You now have a filing system that works.

```
Active files = Main drawer
                Nearest you
Inactive files = Archive drawers
                Farther away
```

So far with every corporation I have worked with, literally every client has expressed that this system is the best they have ever seen and continues to work for them.

Refer back to "The Desk" where I talk about the FileMAP® and now set up your categories using three inch plastic tabs for labeling your files. These categories will mirror your work processes and also will be the same categories you use when organizing your computer files.

ORGANIZE YOUR DESK DRAWER SUPPLIES!

Now we tackle those small supplies that very few know what to do with. Realize the reason you have had trouble in the past in organizing your files and paperwork is because you lack training. Organization is a skill and it must be learned. I had a man call me from an office in Maryland who asked me to come help organize his office. He said he had a mountain of paperwork on his desk, so I told him it would take about eight hours to do his whole office. Now everybody tells me they have a mountain of paperwork on their desk, *but this man really did.* When he went behind his desk and sat down, he disappeared. I walked up to the desk, got on my tiptoes, looked over the mountain of papers and said, "How do you write?"

He said, "I just stand up."

I asked, "Where's your phone?"

He replied, "Lady, I just wait for it to ring."

As I began to analyze his situation, I observed something over his lap that was covered with papers. I couldn't figure out what it was. I thought maybe it was a new type of desk. Much to my amazement, I found out it was his lap drawer. "Don't you need your lap desk drawer?"

"Well, I haven't yet."

"When was the last time you saw that drawer?" I asked.

"Seven years ago," he replied.

We began digging out, and after four hours I was one-quarter finished and had uncovered papers from 1978. This was 2010. This man was in serious trouble and couldn't effectively function in his job.

GOING BACK TO THE 5-STEP PROCEDURE:

1) REMOVE–everything from all your small drawers. Use the floor and...

2) SORT–all items. Simply lay out all your stationery, Xerox paper, clips, pens, pencils, notebook paper, umbrella, keys, McDonald's ketchup and mustard packets, etc. into their proper groups.

3) ELIMINATE–put those items that go someplace else in a box, take them back to the supply cabinet and throw away all those extras you don't need.

4) CONTAIN–all supplies. Use small drawer dividers or baskets.

5) ASSIGN–those supplies a particular drawer, one drawer for stationery, one drawer for pads, one drawer for utensils, etc. The large supplies, like Xerox paper or big boxes of stationery, go on your shelving. (Refer to Books/Resources/Large Supplies.)

ORGANIZE YOUR LOOSE PAPERS!

Now for all those loose papers that are strung out all over your desk, credenza and floor, you need stackables to go on your desktop. **Remove.** Pick all your papers up and put them in one huge pile. **Sort.** Pick up the first piece of paper and decide what action you will need to take on it. Here is a chart that will help you more quickly make a decision on all those pieces of loose papers. Refer back to the stacks we defined in "The Desk".

When Action Required Is:	Place Paper In:
To do now (this week)	Do now (stackable)
To do later (this month)	Do later (stackable)
To give someone to read	Delegate (stackable)
To read	Clip article and place in "to read" stackable
A bill to pay	To pay stackable
To make a phone call, etc.	To call stackable or to call basket

If you find a piece of paper that actually is part of a project you have in a file, then file the paper right into the existing file. Go through each piece of paper this way until you get to the bottom of the pile. When you finish you will have sorted all your loose papers into one of your stackables or into a file in your file drawers. Now you know where every piece of paper is and you can find each immediately.

ORGANIZE YOUR BOOKS/RESOURCES AND LARGER SUPPLIES!

The key to organizing all your books, resources and larger supplies is to use shelving. I always suggest a minimum of one shelving unit, however it is better if you have two. One unit goes in your office and holds  needed books, manuals, and resources, and the other goes in your closet or another room to hold all your extra supplies.

The five steps to organizing your books and resources are listed previously but let's review them again:

1) Remove all extra supplies from your present storage area.

2) Sort all items in like categories.

3) Eliminate outdated letterhead, old business cards and archive manuals, dried up pens, old magazines, etc.

4) Contain. Put small supplies like pens and clips in small baskets. Put magazines in cardboard magazine holders. Put letterhead and envelopes in stackables so you can access them without having to unstack. Put different colored Xerox® paper in stackables for easy accessibility.

5) Assign these containers and items a place on your shelving unit.

Well, you've done it! Your office is efficient and organized and you feel like a million dollars. Your productivity will skyrocket as well as your self-esteem!

CONQUERING COMPUTER CHAOS

(with John Jenkins | www.reconciliation.com)

One businesswoman grappled with a heavy decision. Should she smash her computer with a sledgehammer or throw on a life jacket to keep her head above the flood of information that barraged her each day?

It wasn't that she didn't appreciate the technology. As a writer, she could transmit her work to any location in the world without leaving her desk. She could communicate with editors and publishers with the click of a mouse. But between the stacks of paper on her desk, the e-mails piling up like Mount Rushmore, and the growing number of files on her hard drive, she was spending between twenty to thirty minutes at the beginning of each day just trying to sort through the mess.

SAVING TIME = SOUND BOTTOM LINE

Did you know the loss of just 20 minutes a day of a $60K per year employee is about $2,200 per year, and for a $120K employee—$4,400 per year. Astounding, isn't it?

How often do we spend twenty minutes tracking down that elusive file saved just last month? What about the time spent figuring out where to put files, how to name files, deciding where to delete files, and time spent recreating files?

In an honest moment, one client said, "I don't spend any time at all looking for files, I just create a new one each time".

Proliferation of new files is not the only problem. Duplicate files are also a major headache for many of our clients. We once assisted a client who had a three-foot stack of 11" x 17" printouts on the floor in his office—paper replicas of information stored on his computer, not to mention duplicates saved in e-mails!

This busy manager used this system because he "didn't have time to organize." Yet he shuffled through that stack up to seven times each day. In a quick test, we timed him at three minutes as he attempted to locate a specific paper report. That meant, on average, he spent over 20 minutes a day looking through the paper stack. He didn't even attempt to locate the reports on his computer.

Using the calculation above, you can see disorganization and duplication of files was costing this man's department and company a princely sum.

What happens to the new employee who must inherit this system?

Employee turnover cost companies thousands of dollars. It is a challenge to take over management of critical files when there is no evident system in place. This cost is far greater than the cost of technology equipment or company-wide technology training for employees. We have found that most companies recoup 100% of organization education investment in less than three months.

INFORMATION IS POWER, OR IS IT?

Someone once said, "information is power", but that is an incomplete statement. It should read, "retrievable information is power".

Due to technology, today we can work faster, communicate better, and store and retrieve vital information. But if this is true, why do employees worldwide feel burdened by technology? One Labor Day survey said that over 80% of employees are stressed by technology: computers, e-mails, fax machines, etc.

So, what is the answer? Toss your computer out the window?

Not yet. In the case of the manager above, we showed him that he could find his files—whether paper or computer—in less than 15 seconds flat. The amount of time needed to organize the reports?

Fifteen minutes! Less than one day's hunting through the stack.

We must change our paradigm from "I don't have the time to be organized" to "I organize to have time!"

THE FILEMAP® SYSTEM

Since 1982 we have worked with large corporations and businesses, as well as individuals and home offices, to organize their files, paperwork and work processes. Because technology is now the tool used for every facet of work, we tweaked our system and came up with the FileMap® System for computer files and paper files.

Our system is so simple that many companies and individuals usually are astounded. When we arrive, we find that many people have braced themselves for an intricate and expensive solution to solve all their problems. But FileMAP® is very simple. Just to review, it stands for the following:

M—MAIN: The files you are now working with
A—ARCHIVES: All your old files and inactive files
P—PERSONAL: Personal files like 401k, Insurance, etc.

GETTING STARTED

The first step is to create a system based on what you do. Most people create files by alphabetizing. But FileMAP® is a system where you organize your files and categories by your work processes. What does that mean? Every part of the file structure is related to what you do, your job function or work processes.

If you are part of a team, file structure and file naming must be created as a team so that if Jane has a family emergency, anyone in that department can step in and retrieve and manage her information.

When we held our first FileMAP® Seminars, we expected a nightmare. We thought there would be a tug of war for individual ideas, but what we found was the exact opposite. Most people desire organization and therefore came quickly together as a team to set up their FileMAP® System.

PUTTING FILEMAP® TO WORK

Once the team determines the common organizing vocabulary—category, file structure, and file names—one of the Main files might look like:

MAIN: Marketing
CATEGORY OR WORK PROCESS: Clients
SUBCATEGORIES: 3M™, IBM®, Microsoft®, Xerox®
SUB-FILES: Letters, Proposals, Projects, Memos, etc.

If you don't use memos, then you wouldn't create a sub-file for memos. Remember, you only set up a system by your work process—what you actually do.

Once you determine this common organizing vocabulary, you use it across the board. Whatever file structure and file names are used for the Main files, the same is used for Archives.

Whenever you are through with a file, it is very simple to retire that file because you move it into the same file structure in Archives. If you ever need to retrieve those inactive files, it is a simple process.

E-MAIL

Organizing e-mails is slightly different than organizing your paper piles, but the concept remains unchanged.

ORGANIZING YOUR E-MAILS

You organize your e-mails very similar to how we taught you to organize your loose papers. The biggest difference between e-mails and loose papers is there's no need to create separate "Delegate" "Do later" and "Do now" folders like we did when organizing loose papers.

You can use your e-mail program to do a lot of this for you. With each e-mail that comes in, ask yourself which of the 3D processes applies. If you need to work on your e-mail right away, then do it now or create a task for the item. If it can wait, schedule time on your calendar or create a task for a later date. Delegated items can be forwarded to the appropriate person, or assigned the task directly, depending on your e-mail program. Your e-mails are now out of your inbox—effectively out of sight, out of mind—but not forgotten.

THROW AWAY THAT SLEDGEHAMMER!

It takes time to organize, but the beauty of developing an organized system for your computer files and e-mails is that it saves time, money, and energy that can be devoted to other worthwhile projects. When you can locate a file within 15 seconds or less, you are no longer faced with frustration that goes hand in hand with disorganization. You might even discover that you no longer have the urge to smash your computer to smithereens, and the computer has become the timesaving tool it was meant to be.

HOW DO I KEEP MY OFFICE MAINTAINED?

This section is full of tips and techniques to keep your office organized. They are energy-givers. If you do them you will gain energy. However, you must do them or your office will slowly slip back into chaos. Here are the ideas.

WORST FIRST. Anytime of the day when you have the choice of three to nine things to do, choose the worst first. That way, you get the worst over first and then you can look forward to doing all those things you enjoy.

ENJOY FIRST. The only exception to the idea above is first thing in the morning. To get energy and look forward to getting up in the morning, spend the first

30 minutes each day doing what you enjoy first (except sleep). Jog, shower, read, or walk. As you get in the habit, your body will start adapting and you will find your early morning a delight.

CLEAR OFF YOUR DESK AT THE END OF EACH DAY. This gives you a feeling of finishing out your day and helps you in the transition to home. It gives you immediate energy when you come into the office in the morning.

WORK ON ONE PROJECT AT A TIME ON THE TOP OF YOUR DESK. Working on more than one project will distract you and you will lose papers more easily. Before starting the second project, put away the first.

PUT THINGS AWAY, NOT DOWN. Did you ever watch the mailman at the post office? Does he take your package and just set it aside to rush on to the next customer? No. First he stamps and then places each package where it is supposed to go. Then he serves the next customer. He is stopping work long enough to put things in their place before he moves on to another customer.

PLAN AND LAY OUT EACH NIGHT WHAT YOU WILL WEAR THE NEXT DAY. This leaves no room for errors. You get up the next day and you don't have to think, it's all laid out for you.

TAKE ONE TO TWO SOLID DAYS TO COMPLETELY ORGANIZE YOUR OFFICE BEFORE YOU START WORK. Whatever time you invest in organizing you will get back in time saved.

ORGANIZING IS SHARPENING YOUR AX AND CONTINUOUSLY REFINING YOUR SYSTEM. To organize properly, you must stop your normal work routine to do it.

END YOUR DAY ON A NOTE OF ACCOMPLISHMENT. Don't fire an employee or reprimand anyone at the end of the day. Also, work on the most enjoyable project at the very end of the day.

RUNNING ERRANDS. Always plan your route and while driving try to take only right turns. Left turns will take an extra 3 minutes per turn. Plan your route and save time and money.

WHEN YOU TRAVEL. Try to return the end of the day or leave at least one-half day to answer your calls, do your paperwork, write expense reports, answer your mail and do your laundry.

EAT NUTRITIONALLY. Eat light lunches and avoid alcohol.

EXERCISE. Briskly walk, jog, bicycle, or do some type of exercise every day that works your heart up to a fast pace for 15 minutes.

KEEP YOUR FAMILY LIFE AND WORK LIFE BALANCED. Remember, if it's not working at home, eventually it will fall apart at work. Make it a rule to take off one whole day out of every seven days. This is a fantastic time management trick that literally will save you money, energy and time.

One day off totally refreshes you for the following week, increasing energy and productivity as well as enhancing your family life.

Keep your office a model for others to copy. You are in control and have extra time to spend on the most important areas of your life, your family.

Take some time to reassess what is your top priority and

> Organization is
> a skill and it
> must be learned.

I am quite sure that you will realize that the reason you need to become more organized is because you value your time and want to spend it with those that mean the most to you.

When your life is about to end and you look back on all your accomplishments and failures, the one thing you will wish for is that you had spent more time with your family and closest loved ones. Make today the first day of the rest of your life - make that commitment to take the extra time that you have gained and invest that time in your family and friends.

I guarantee you will not regret it.

REMEMBER: You will never have time to organize, you organize to have time.

APPENDICES

PARADIGM SHIFT REVIEW

ORGANIZATIONAL COMPARISON

OFFICE ORGANIZATION REVIEW

TEAR OUT SUPPLY CHECKLIST

PARADIGM SHIFT REVIEW

PARADIGM #1	"I don't have time to organize."	"I organize to have time."
PARADIGM #2	"I am constantly un-stacking stuff to get to stuff."	"Don't go through your work to get to your work."
PARADIGM #3	"I can never seem to finish anything. I get distracted so easily."	"Finish fully a project or finish a portion of what you start."
PARADIGM #4	"I'll just put it here in case I need it... I'll just stick it here for now."	"Put things away, not down."
PARADIGM #5	"If only I had more space... If I just had a bigger house... If only I had more..."	"Focus on wanting what you have, not having what you want."
PARADIGM #6	"I never have any time for myself. Work never seems to stop. I haven't been in the bathroom alone since last February."	"Keep the Sabbath 'Wholly.' Take off one whole day every week by incorporating the concept of a Sabbath into your schedule."

PARADIGM SHIFT REVIEW

PARADIGM #7	"I have so much stuff, but I can't seem to let any of it go."	"When you buy something new, give away two."
PARADIGM #8	"It just seems I am constantly plagued by little irritants that absorb my time and eat up my day."	"Organize your environment by removing small irritants that hinder your achievement."
PARADIGM #9	"Stuff is everywhere. I can never find anything."	"Assign a place for everything. Give everything a home."
PARADIGM #10	"If I don't do it, who will?"	"Never do for others what they can do for themselves."
PARADIGM #11	"Organization just doesn't work for me. I straighten up my office many times, but it just doesn't stay."	"Organization is not straightening, neatening, or rearranging. Organization is establishing a system."
PARADIGM #12	"I don't know where to start."	"Think S.T.A.R.T. Start Today an Action to Reach your Target."

PARADIGM SHIFT REVIEW

PARADIGM #13	"I have so much to do, I will never get it all done."	"Divide and conquer. Remember, home (and office) weren't built in a day"
PARADIGM #14	"If I can just get these little jobs out of the way, I'll have the time to focus on what's really important."	"Do the most important project at the beginning of the day."
PARADIGM #15	"I need a large clump of time to start a project. It's all or nothing with me. If I can't find three hours for this project, I'll never get it done."	"Break larger projects into smaller time segments, doable throughout the day, to reduce idle time."
PARADIGM #16	"I just don't have enough time."	"You have all the time there is."
PARADIGM #17	"If I file it, I will never find it. Out of sight, out of mind."	"It's not the filing you fear, nor is it the out-of-sight, out-of-mind; it's the lack of a system."

PARADIGM SHIFT REVIEW

PARADIGM #18	"When I was growing up, I had so little that I want my kids never to experience the poverty that I went through."	"Focus on giving your kids what you have, instead of focusing on providing them with what you didn't have."
PARADIGM #19	"But if I clear off my desk, it will look like I don't have any work."	"A cleared desk is a sign of efficiency and effectiveness."
PARADIGM #20	"Getting organized will constrain me or confine me."	"Real order liberates."
PARADIGM #21	"Getting organized doesn't help, cause I will never stay organized. I will just mess it up, and it will fall back into chaos."	"Once you are organized, spend only one minute per hour of every day maintaining the organization."

ORGANIZATIONAL COMPARISON

ENVIRONMENT	WORK HABITS	SPIRIT
Assign special areas for your possessions.	Sharpen your axe.	Respond to your season in life.
Prepare yourself and your environment for its greatest efficiency.	Do right things as well as do things right.	Guard diligently your priorities.
Take care of what you own to extend its usefulness.	Know your limitation, by recognizing co-workers' and spouse's strengths.	Know your purpose in life.
Remove obstacles that hinder your achievement.	Develop standards, fences, and boundaries.	Keep the Sabbath 'Wholly.' Take off one whole day every week by incorporating the concept of a Sabbath into your schedule."
Simplify your lifestyle by sharing with others.	Be content with your present lifestyle.	
Being ORGANIZED IN YOUR ENVIRONMENT means being able to find and easily get to what you own.	Reject distractions that hinder you from reaching your goals.	Being ORGANIZED IN YOUR SPIRIT means being able to live in consistent rest and contentment.
	Being ORGANIZED IN YOUR WORK HABITS means you will be more productive in your workday.	

OFFICE ORGANIZATION REVIEW

REMOVE	The very first step would be to remove all the stuff.
SORT	As you are removing all items, sort according to like items.
ELIMINATE	You can eliminate. You either throw them directly into the trash or you have a box labeled to go elsewhere.
CONTAIN	Put each group in a container, a drawer divider, or a shallow box before you place them back in the drawer.
ASSIGN	Assign those containers a defined place in the drawer.

THE FILEMAP® SYSTEM

MAIN	These are the files that you are now working on, they are actively a part of your job.
ARCHIVE	All other files that do not fit in your Main drawer go into your Archive drawers.
PERSONAL	This drawer contains all your personal files, like your insurance papers, your pay stubs, or your 401K or evaluations.

STACKABLES

1) Do Now is this week

All papers you know you will have to do this week go into that stackable.

2) Do Later is this month

You need to do this, but it probably won't get done this week but needs to be looked at this month.

3) Delegate is this person

Whomever you consistently delegate work to needs a stackable. The delegate stackable can also hold papers that you need to discuss with your co-workers

OTHER STACKABLES

4) To Read
5) To Pay
6) To Call
7) To File
8) In-box
9) Out-box

REMEMBER: You will never have time to organize, you organize to have time.

TEAR-OUT SUPPLY CHECKLIST

	File Cabinet		Pencil Sharpener
	Clips		Pens
	Computer/Printer		Markers
	Copier		Postage Scale
	Dictionary/Thesaurus		Postcards
	Stackable Trays		Post-it® Notes
	Drawer Dividers		Rubber Bands
	Fax Machine		Scissors
	File Folders		Small Baskets/Boxes for Supplies
	Glue		Stamps
	Labels		Stapler/Staple Remover
	Labels (Pre-Addressed)		Staples
	Mailing Envelopes		Stationery
	Notebook		Tape and Dispenser
	Pads		Telephone
	Paper		Trash Can
	Pencils		White-Out Fluid

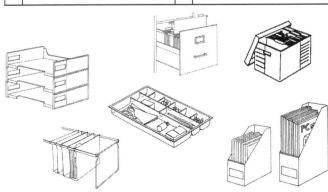

Sue McMillin
Professional Organizer
Motivational Speaker

WHAT WE DO
Since 1982, Sue McMillin has helped her clients develop strategies for organizing their work so that they can get more done, make more money, and have more time to focus on what matters most. This is accomplished through seminars and personal coaching.

BENEFITS
Sue's trademarked FileMAP® System will dramatically improve individual and group organizational skills, enabling her clients to find anything they own in seconds, recover 40% space in their environment, gain up to an hour a day, eliminate clutter, increase professionalism, turbo-charge creativity and save up to $5,000/employee/year of gained productivity.

WE WANT TO HEAR FROM YOU
Send Sue an e-mail at Sue@WithTimeToSpare.com and tell her about your journey to a clutter-free lifestyle.

PRAISE FOR SUE MCMILLIN'S LIFE-CHANGING SEMINARS

"The enthusiasm for the project grew by the hour... a side benefit was a feeling of teamwork ... Your 'Clutter Therapy' really works!"

—Richard C., Trane®

"I am a much more productive person...I no longer waste time looking through stacks...thanks for providing us some tools"

—Sandy H., Human Resources Director,
Georgetown Medical

"You imparted to us a system that will forever change the way we do our jobs. I gained a powerful tool that will enable me to be more effective, more focused, and more valuable to my company."

—Julie V., Director, Gannett

E-MAIL
Sue@WithTimeToSpare.com

WEB
www.WithTimeToSpare.com

Made in the USA
Lexington, KY
07 June 2014